The Wild Dance of the Hunted Gypsy

Zoe Williamson

Order this book online at www.trafford.com
or email orders@trafford.com

Most Trafford titles are also available at major online book retailers.

Print information available on the last page.

ISBN: 978-1-4907-6558-7 (sc)
ISBN: 978-1-4907-6557-0 (e)

Trafford rev. 10/22/2015

 www.trafford.com

North America & international
toll-free: 1 888 232 4444 (USA & Canada)
fax: 812 355 4082

GRATITUDE

For those hungered and resolute
outcasts and the untamed
of nomadic tread, and wanderers
artists and poets.....to each of us, unswerving, determined, unwavering
I ask only once, set free the universe.......

DEDICATIONS

To my children of everfl owing wisdom
and unfolding colours no other fl owers can equal
To my husband of kuon ganjo,
who makes sense to the unbelievable

Finding the mystical connection across universe is to discover even buddhas fall in love.
It exists therefore,
In the eyes of the beloved fortune appears

INTRODUCTION

This is to those in love and in search of, whom have crossed oceans and minefields, lifetimes embroiled with obstacles and hardships, embittered and poignant, of those refused and undefeated, of those who with hearts filled with passions overflowing of a faith profound and embedded. Of fervour and ardent belief, optimism flourishes from a body brimming with courageous effort creating a value of immense fortune. Watering the passions of everyone around, the environment blossoms in health and vibrant energy, this is to those who will never give up. That on the brink of nothing else but to survive, their very breath respires with the universe, summoning possibilities that had far been out of reach to the disconcerted. This is for those disbelieved, discredited, the hunted and untamed, For the pierced and hurt, the alone and the deserving, This is for those unsung, of agonies invisible, of those relentless and striving, This is for those who love, whose hearts are full, set free the universe.....This is time to begin our dance …..

OF PASSIONS, TRUE MAGIC AND WONDER

To the heart of my passions and all my desires, the answer to my dreams, the reason and meaning to each sunrise and the beauty at each suns descent, the bright beauty from the moon, and to the man who knows me, feels me, and wants me...... I am everlastingly his forever and always way past the edge of a time that will begin again and so remain his, because it is constant and limitless, and I love him and breathe him, smell him and sense him, I feel his Daimoku, and bathe in his wisdom. He makes love to me at every conceivable moment, and my body belongs alongside his. Warm and comforted, he has no equal, and there are none who could try.

And then imagine this man I write to and of and dream of endlessly, carry him with me to each corner of my life and how it unfolds as a mystical rose of unknown indescribable beauty....

know he does exist and will forever more, my heart expands and yearns and beats with undying passions.... resounding as do the drums of the distant past that encountered us both on a morning before first dawn.

He creates in me all things magic and sends trembling shimmers of absolute ecstasy throughout my body into my outer memories inscribing the stars in love spun glimmers,

he visits by nightime, the call of the moon guides his love to me and I wrap myself into the silky blankets that hug my body, smooth over my skin.

I imagine these are his desirous fingers in discovery of my wanting body rhythmically moving to his touch. I miss him so much I send my thoughts of sensuous dreams to the moon for her to shower upon him in his nightime, so he can stretch along the covers of his matress in reach of me and find me.

Loving him, Wanting him. Wanting him to feel the same.

Believing in him and allowin g him knowledge he is the love of my life, and shines the brightest of all illuminations, and by the magic of the most careful hands, inscribe his name into the constellations.

Where he is now is within me, all around me, in me and all about, somewhere near and yet seperated by miles in their thousands and yet so close, but where my heart resides is within his own. I feel his heart beat fiercely, and his passion flow across the beautiful braided heart connection. A connection of kuon ganjo, of interlinked promises sent and pledged against the backdrops of greater worlds....to remember each other in a union of a golden future, somewhere along the mystic, centred into the flaming horizon. A place where no eyes can steal themselves away from untold beauty as it spreads across the endless, monumentous skies, the heart of promises, where all whom have ever loved realize the songs of the beloved. His heart nectar sweetened by impassioned hope. He is of comfort to the bitterness of life, unsweetened and cruel, that can soothe the darkest secrets that crawl about one's mind......accompanying me now upon a stretch of ten thousand lifetimes and more beyond the silkiness of graceful aging, carrying the years with a certainty, a reassurance that each moment lived, each second kissed, brings us closer and I feel, I feel him ....

and how he whispered to me further than the profoundest secrets that keep their dances amongst the glistening constellations,

"I will take you there,
wait for me
Into the heart of the mystic rests the impossible.....
our journey is just beginning
…...it exists....".

WHEN THE MOON LIGHTS THE SKY IN SILVER

Inspired by moon's arrival, she lights up the night in silver,
Spills stardust upon the dreams caught up by the breezes.......
.....when the thought of our heart partner illuminates the blackest dark..
..where the mountains have been climbed
And there are more yet, undiscovered, in view against the horizon backdrop...
Recollections of a time lived, a future of endless beginnings...
Of composition and heart connections..... since kuon ganjo I wonder how much further I can
go, but then there is the entire universe...
And the essence of the air is such freedom.
Sunrise and good fortune rising, gracious of mystical wonder..
Sweet paradise found in one morning
found in him where my heart is home.
And from rain and sunshine, spring hope, Great hope.....
with no doubt at all
In a hundred million years would I relinquish my feelings for you
You find your way to me through the deepest hardships
too precious you are my king
Because in you where passion is discovered
Possibilities unfold
And opportunities blossom.....
Refresh the skies, and dance the eternal,
Nurture my body, nourish my soul,
Allow freedom in my wings,
And sail the skies into the unknown with him.

There is a song of the beloved, the universe whispers in response .....
he is the beauty all about me, I become the magic he makes me feel..

CHERISHED HOPE

I summon those challenges
Entice them to me
Beckon them
I must show them

because nothing can foil a love so profound
It has become embedded into the rocks that formed the Earth
Into the mountains, the rolling waves of the sea,
Withion everything he is,
And is everything to me.

I am in everything, and everywhere,
I cannot be destroyed.
To forsake all else,
My spirit lives...
They cannot revile me,
Though they try to hunt me...
Do not tame the wild,
They cannot be broken...
I am in you,
I am all around you,
I am with you,
I live in you.

ON EVERLASTING LOVE

Render me deeply within the confines
of a heart
That encapsulates a passion aflame
with the desires
That have embroidered themselves into the breeze of eternal life
To feel
To know
To sense him in each fibre of my living body

To smell him at waking morning moments
Taste him apart from dreams
From a tongue that craves the cream of his passion
Embrace his form coming alive inside me

There is a moment of beauty that begins
at the innocence of each day born,

As I understood the meanings to each morning,
the sun drew breath, the planets aligned,
and the horizon shimmered gold,
to be part of this summoned such excitement...

I knew then that in every moment that passed
would contain a prayer
made from a time elapsed into the spectrum of time
that flowed inside me

With each year that crept along
and with it stealing a youth that allowed to be taken
Because within the experience of aging grace
Was born new years dripping in vibrant spirit

Blue light turning swiftly to gold
By window frame into silver light
Spun by stars
inscribed by love
Written into the magical dance of two loving bodies

The rhythm shared by you and I
A unique response to a lifetime of prayers

Spun from a heartbeat

As if in mantric resonance, repeated over and over

Int ime with a fidelity that remains obedient
To one heart so full
bursting almost with a furious extravangance of desire

It was futility to compare to another
A lifeless inability to ever wonder further
That no one other could compare

None are there my love
that could compare to the beauty of you

of victory and great wonder
Of longing and heart connection

And of passion, the willingness of my body against yours,
of moistened embrace
And lips that respond in spoken embrace

Each time of tongue as if inscribed
along our mystical thread
spun from my loving heart to your own

Yet to utter these words once
Does not satisfy the world of my desire
As if by mantric trance
I repeat over and over
My prince I love you I love you I love you.

I bathe in gratitude
Awash in desire
To have travelled the length of a mystical thread without end
Of years and lifetimes
of miles and miles to get into you
In you my eternal prince resides the sun.

A warmth of inexplicable joy
Inscribed from innocent passions
aflame from my heart to yours
Unite with me my love
My prince, my beloved king,
In moistened bliss
To know I love him
How much I love him
To spread my wings and feel the sunshine
To dance in the radiance of his rays

To allow him knowledge
To embrace every part of him,

I cannot say enough I love you I love you I love you........

Tiger turn to me,
Tread closely by me,
Open wide your heart let them hear you
Jump into my heart ....

She turns to face the arbitrary tongue...
and from deep inside she summons a passion so full, so powerful,
frighteningly loud it deafens the skies..........
and she roars.

DREAMS OF THE HUNTED GYPSY

To the heart of my passions
The pulse of my desires,
The only answer to my dreams,
Bringing reason and meaning to each sunrise

For beauty at each suns descent,
The brightest beauty from the moon,
Is to the man who knows me, feels me, and wants me......

I am everlastingly his forever and always
I am his on an everlasting promise.

Way past the edge of a time that begins again and again,
I remain his, because it is constant and limitless,
I love him and breathe him, smell him and sense him,
In his prayer, bathed in his wisdom.

He makes love to me at every conceivable moment,
My body belongs alongside his.
Warm and comforted, he has no equal, and there are none who could try.

And so imagine this man I dream of endlessly,
carry him with me to each corner of my life
Watch how it unfolds as a mystical rose of unknown indescribable beauty could....
know he does exist and will forever more,

my heart expands and yearns and beats with undying passions....

resounding as do the drums of the distant past that encountered us both on a morning before
first dawn.

He creates in me all things magic and sends trembling shimmers of absolute ecstasy throughout
my body

he visits by nightime,

the call of the moon guides his love to me

I wrap myself into the silky blankets that hug my body,

smooth over my skin.

I imagine these are his desirous fingers

In discovery of my wanting body

rhythmically moving to his touch.

I miss him so much I send my thoughts of sensuality to the moon

for her to shower upon him in his nightime,

so he can stretch along the covers of his mattress in reach of me and find me.

Loving him, Wanting him.

Believing in him safe in the knowledge he knows he is the love of my life,

and shines the brightest of all illuminations,

and by the magic of the most careful hands, inscribe his name into the constellations.

Where he is now I have no idea,
but where my heart resides is within his own.
I feel his heart beat fiercely,
and his passion flows across the beautiful braided heart connection.
His heart nectar sweetened by impassioned hope.
Once more the song resounds inside me

Again and again I hear those melodies circle my ears
I cried for the heartbreak
I anguished when he was taken from me
But I remained true to my promise

I am his because if not for him

then who then tell me who
It was he who whispered one golden sunrise
When our world was in flames

"If not for you my sweet love
then why does my heartbeat still if not for you."

I am his on an everlasting promise
I remembered when I found him that day
I clasp my hands in fervour
day after day after day.

He is seen in the clearest sunsets
When the clouds have disappeared

The moon moves into full view,
allowing her pure beauty to extend

To the broken heart of one so tender,

So gentle and pure with love of

the absolute, of the enamoured…..

Embracing messages to the heart of

crystal until the next time,

Upon their song,

"If not in this lifetime, then I will see you in the next"

The moon bore witness that

one night before the heart of his princess broke
His messages of undying, everlasting

love finally sunk into her, and she drank from his courage, his kindness

spilling over into her eyes that filled with tears of immense hope…..

"I must leave you now in this lifetime

But my love I will search for you upon the next"

He touched her skin as soft as the still waters
And buried his face into her hair,
""I rise up against my demons I blossom in a hundred different colours, do not lose

me, I will not be gone
It is only now we are unallowed, it is only this time

Find me again, I will know you
Search me once more

I will believe in you
I will always live in your heart ….........

I will protect your dreams
I will journey your life…….
Do not lose me,
I will not be gone"

To the heart of my passions
The pulse of my desires,
The only answer to my dreams,
Bringing reason and meaning to each sunrise

Is to the man who knows me, feels me, and wants me……

HELD IN HIS ARMS

And there is no greater gift
than to be adorned in his grace

His hands hold me
closing me tightly to his side

I have danced a million years of wonder
I have sung a million years in harmony with him,
And how oceans have crashed
Waves of turmoil thrashed into one another

If galaxies have collided and died to be reborn again
If creation opens new horizons into further horizons
onto distant celestial plateaus against what cannot be explained

Matters not......

I have stood upon shorelines over lifetimes and lifetimes
counting our fortunes paved in golden sands
inscribing love upon ever moving grounds
shaking under irrevocable mundial changes

My dance to the beloved is of him,
Instep with my beloved,
because to dance with him,
Is the eternal whisper of the universe,
Is the next breath inside me,
becomes the very pulse under my skin,
My heartbeat within his,
My lips upon his.........

In union born again and again I pledge to be.....
Always his, indeed there is no greater gift,
my reflection in his eyes.

Love that has been buried deep so many centuries, past so much millenia
had lain dormant within
Awoken only to your loveliness
My body and the very essence of my soul came alive
the instant my eyes rested upon yours.

Listen closely as 1000 voices crescendo each second, each moment
Expounding the universe
and there is nothing that will keep me from you
No matter how we are prevented......

My love true, hear my heart speaking,
Each fibre of my being awakened to this mystical touch
Moving me to the place I wish to be.
How dreams can flourish
Hope never darkens....

these voices cry from the wild
Into the song of the untamed
It is the chorus of the hunted.....
A call along the mystic...I hear you,
My love, I hear you.

Glide on past the silky smooth pathway across blazened skies of inidgo violet
Hear the hum of the universe
follow the songs of the stars
Watch how each glittering heartbeat sparkles on endless
of those beloved, of those loved forever........

HONEY OF THE LOTUS

Honey of the Lotus
Honey so very deep within my soul
Careful prayers sent as dreams to the beloved
Upon mystical moon
Silver radiant, travel from my edge to his....

Stay with me, he says until the sunset eternity
I will meet you once more
Await the jewel encrusted turtle tailed Eagle dragon
Step upon his feathered back and hold tight
As you cross the fires of the horizon flickering gentle
Embers of the sunset now silent....

This is the cry of the wild
and a calling along the mystic.
A sweeter honeyed youth everlasting
because we will not die amongst the usual

Although distant your body warms me
Await the silver, jewelled Eagle dragon
Whom will glide you across the silver array ceiling
glistening bright.
A radiance of magical diamonds,
sparkling mystical....
"I will not leave you."

Honey of the Lotus
Honey so very deep within my soul
Careful prayers sent as dreams to the beloved
Upon mystical moon
Silver radiant, travel from my edge to his....

In a place where we allow the universe to listen and in return summon our unwavering trust, a story is told of lifetimes past, a dream recurred and in unabated fashion appeared once more to my recipient, and history unfolded, a romance was discovered..... and inspired the following, from his words into mine.....

DREAMS UPON THE MYSTIC

Along the thread of the mystic

I have loved you next to the gentlest winds

Against the milder breezes blowing

Across the softest spring sunrise…

Oh my prince I have always been inside you

I hold onto your words and treasure soft passion

Like the fragility of snowdrops,

The velvet touch of a sensual rose

The softer bloom of fuscias……

Against the voluminous backdrop that hurts us

Your song comes alive inside…..

Your heart beats at pace with mine,

Against mine, against time…..

Uncertain reality takes form in the mountainous universe of a time so

long ago in an existence way past the beginning of all beginnings…

Since then the skies have since turned over and stars reformed, and *where a brilliant sun shone once lay the embers of flickers, and new*

moons in search of partner planets to rest their pull.

Far from the surrounds where we make home in the nowadays reality

becomes an existence of countless possibilities where cries a subtle

sound of faraway wonders and openings into the surreal as we might

see it, but it is a finer land of edgeless potentialities....

In a home so close to our hearts where resides such impassioned

feelings unallowed to manifest from infinite pasts way past all beginnings

to a moment of space where life was ruled against our hearts, further

than horizons that permitted us to dream, begins a story of love

unlimited without doubt, a love that persevered and prospered.

To the chagrin of those persecutors, and they that might have loved themselves

this endurance of love everlasting.

One man remained constant and on a pledge of mortal endurance,

broke from the bonds of regulation

to admit to his seeking heart that the goodness that flowed from her

wholeness, was the nectar he so desired, that irretrievably could only be

a sustenance from her only she could satisfy.

Where in the folds of promises pledged in silence from unworded

passion, a love was born of Kuon Ganjo, because it had always existed

and continued to flow as does the Mystical river of the infinite of where

we are all born

Thus an illicit world of tendered affections and mutual passion was

birthed, secret from the piety that encapsulated their daily lives.

The very sun and moon and stars, the entire universe as it shone

through, bore witness to their intense emotions unfolding, the skies

turned indigo violet and the planets aligned to synchronize such unique

tendresses....beauty uprising, love impassioned with flames that would

not be tamed......

Over 5000 years ago he lived as an artist and painted at the Emperors

pleasure and she, a concubine, of his Imperial pleasure.

And those who with unfailing loyalty would even surpass their own

lives, would avail to encourage this courtship of uneven and precarious

tread.....

And yet in the harsh regimes of an ancient world of a

far Eastern land, they found a happiness in their confinement, a freedom borne of their hearts.

A passion that burst forth and embraced them, each kiss a pledge of renewed love.....

and so they would begin their adventures under the emerald trees

with leaves to bright and wide, there they would meet and clasp hands

running wildly into newer horizons in wait....

In each others eyes...reflected a depth of unity inexplicable, beyond

any comprehension they had ever known, at the first sighting precious,

unmistakable moments of fragile realizations, beauty incarnate, gracious

undertakings of deep affections known before. From kenzoku spirited

souls that have met somewhere in the long ago unknown...they make

home in one another, whom they have longed for and yearned, whispered

softly to know and become part of....

Such a love so impassioned regardless....

Yet came a braver future where they made plans to elope under the

hood of the fullest moon, and on that night they would disappear from

the world of brutal regime forever.

And through fear that came washing through them, regardless their

hearts were aflame and ignited the sun as it rose lifting dawn high into

the sky.

Undefeated they would be, as a lotus unfolding amidst muddy waters.

Becoming the colours that blend rose streaked lilac skies in radiance

at each others wonder…how fierce these flames burn and cannot

die…they have continued to set fire to the horizon since the earth

began…

To swim in the magnificence of love, before unknown a pleasure of

depth unspoken, hands clasped tightly.. for the night was seemingly

trepid

And yet this fear if it existed was humble

A feeling witnessed by them only and by the truth of a lovers kiss

He would paint her breathlessly into each sunrise

And she in return sing her song" along the thread of the mystic

I have loved you next to the gentlest winds

Against the milder breezes blowing

Across the softest spring sunrise…

Oh my prince I have always been inside you"

Who could know of a delivery of deceit, and of bloodthirsty actions and

greed for the honour of his master' approval, to hunt the lovers and those in love, who might dare to quash their affections…..

who might

drip his poison onto the carpet of the Imperial Emperor, with sly grin and

wanton vengeance seek to pierce the heart filled with timeless nectar

from two hearts braver than he could possibly imagine.

To the chagrin of the open hearted the fearful slinking foe of the most

woeful must rear its head and perform devilish functions

And with trust broken to pieces his many faces turned in unison to

greet the lovers with a hand of friendship that turned into the black

sodden leaves of the rose that had died days before, and betrayed their

betrothel….

as he steered the boat that had offered a hope of freedom,

that would once have taken them to safer

shores and away from the flashing swords that awaited them.

In line with the hand of the betrayer

And our prince, the artist of unfailing love and such impassioned

determination, was dragged from the arms of his beloved to his concrete

cold domain of chains and torture…. And no more would she see him and or wait for him in secret.

Still under the pale coloured emerald trees she would descend the stone palace steps,

awaiting a promise,

touching bark,

tracing his inscriptions, a heart so perfectly carved so deep into the

gentle wood …. And cry softly his return….igniting a flame of cherished

hope so profound within her…..

And he, in an agony unsurpassing any he had come to know before cried out to the

stone walls that bound him

"I rise up against my demons I blossom in a hundred different colours, do not lose

me, I will not be gone"

And so take with this the illumination of loves profundity.

And pledges made against the mists that protect the sun as it sets along

the finest horizon, the mists that continue on and on into an eternal

breath of life's wisdom, that within the beating hearts of two, whom

breathe in each other's nectar, that flows as necessity from the fastening

of one heart to the other,

Still he is seen in the clearer sunsets when the clouds have disappeared and move the moon into full view, allowing her pure beauty to extend

to the broken hearts of one so tender, so gentle and pure with love of

the absolute, of the enamoured…..embraces messages to the bosom of

crystal until the next time,

Upon their song,

"If not in this lifetime, then I will see you in the next"

There is immeasurable pain in heartache however it manifests, and all too soon

the agonizing confusion pierces like a needle to the most vulnerable, the most

tenderhearted….to suffer is too common an occurrence, and yet ….. he returns to

the waiting, a hero, does appear.

His adventure is not written, he is born to free the spirit, to leave her untamed.

His tread is gentle, as his words soft, and he has eyes as full as the heart that

bleeds…….he has love that swims through his veins, and his is a friendship to the

improbable, to the unseen, he embraces the unknown……. He is empathy to the

raining songs of heartbreak.

He is a thousand dreams………

And she could possibly live forever on a radiant stretch of violet celeste amidst the

dawning skies…

"I am yours on an everlasting promise"

IMPRESSIONS OF MAKING THE INCREDULOUS A POSSIBILITY

I cannot describe the feelings that spun through me on that night of the mystic but I breathed in the swirling goodness and filled myself with the beauty that had begun inside me, on an evening that travelled back further than my memories would allow.

I slept adrift the clouds, upon mountain tops dressed in creatures inhabiting the quiet enclosures only some of us allow to set free. It was a time I had lived but cannot recall and yet imprinted within my heart. We spoke in a language of different tongues a dialect of ancient silk. You have forever been a part of the journey and we have travelled further and for the love I feel for you

The angels have sung your graces you sleep under the crystal illumination the psychic watchtower that has guided me through years of unrest and turbulence to be at your side and I embrace your waters. All this makes sense because of the man who pledges his heart to me.

THE MYOHO KING AND THE MYSTICAL DANCE OF THE UNRELENTING PRINCESS

So precious in its imaginings
A world where the worthy and knowing exist
Where the silver lotus birds greet the sunrise
and the hunted gypsy has been kissed.

And imagine too a fine king, handsome, and knowing,
Living on top of a high up mountain shrouded in clouds
that glistened each bright sunny morning.
For whatever the weather it stood wise and proud.

The sun shone so brightly in his presence
His heart was a knowledge profound, and true
With a nectar of such unlimited supply,
even the coldest of hearts could be renewed.

He inscribed verses of love into the eternal
He sang the brightest illuminations across the sky
His fingers touched keys that chimed in resonance
With a wonder that filled passion in his eyes

He shared and offered this as a great gift to the world
So perfect, enough and plentiful for everyone
It beat so rhythmically into the pure essence of morning
And continued in lullaby by the twilight of the sun.

Opening each morning were skies of untold brilliance
Crimsons and deep violets that colour gold
Into magnificent displays of pastels and gentle greens
until the brightest blue flooded the top of the world

All at once birds of splendour would commence their day,
encircling each other, and gliding in unfolding delight
Where he walked small blossoms began to bud,
and when he smiled, droplets of colours began to ignite.

He played a harp made of musical passion,
carved from deft hands, loving, steady and kind,
Of a courageous heart, he sounded drums that echoed through the universe
the sweetest melodies heard from afar and wide

And did he know, oh goodness, could he know
That across the vast ocean of tossing, curling waves
There lived a princess in a world so different from the king
whom danced to the harmonies his sweet hands played.

She lived as princess to the wildest,
and danced to a sound she could not explain.
She sang alongside the hunted, and tormented,
She moved to a beauty found inside the most poignant pain.

Her body constantly moved to the beat she heard from within,
wisps of a flautist, playing endless songs of love
and from these notes she caught kisses
and spoke to the moon, and threw them to the stars above.

Sending them forward into the universe
for the lips that might receive them well,
Because what greater fortune to behold
Would be a beginning ready to unveil.

She sensed the clouds burst into new clouds,
and a strange rhythm broke across the earth.
Where she trod, small blossoms began,
her feet skipped and kicked in gentle worth.

Promises that had been pledged in silence
She recalled whispers under moonlit skies
in lifetimes far away in a time before the mountains grew so tall,
Familiar softness spoken from the wise..

Where different suns shone together onto worlds of magnificence
Where into the autumnal twilights such animals hibernate
Yet in fact stole themselves away inside the earth,
Away from human eyes, to rejoice and celebrate

Away from those who refused to celebrate the moon,
And so to talk and sing, and listen in awe
for stories that unfolded throughout the night
From the princess upon her silver unicorn.....

Revealing secrets of the vows of heart lovers
promises of the beloved in continued spinning
She spoke of the resonance she felt in harmony yet did not know,
but had loved since the edge of all beginnings.

She wrote upon the moon one evening,
To the gentle king inscribing her largest passions
Sweet silver crystal, she cried, from my heart into his
let him know that it happens:

"I follow you into the everlasting sunrise
that becomes our greatest tomorrow.
With you I ride out across blankets of blue sky embracing fortune
and with you I know no more of sadness and sorrow.

And of you, I hold close the golden promise we sang
Whispered when secrets were prominent and young
our love making a silent pledge for eternity., and further
Witnessed and guarded by the eternal sun

.....across the windy reaches of our lifetimes since,
a journey arduous and cruel, and then to feel;
A love that began to fill me with inexplicable joy,
A place inside me, known and not forgotten and real."

She was shaken awake, so tenderly, so gently, by steady hands,
Her eyes opened to the most beautiful sight.
"You, my king were the music I heard each evening
upon the still, silent silver moon that rose every night.

For hundreds of years, you are the melody of the universe,
and sewn into the breezes of mystical fortune, you are my king.
I remember the vows we laid down together in a place
Before beginnings existed........ my truelove everlasting."

She had been crowned with tiara made from star fallen jewels
Those who understood the moon could see
She ran the streets and countryside until her breath vanished inside her
she danced rhythmically to his sweet melody.

She moved and swirled and turned and danced
to the fortunes playing inside her heart.
The king she knew began a symphony of profusion
To unite them and to never be apart.

With this she would ask that he would join her
that they would be inseperable as moon and earth
his voice resounded round his flutes and pipes
Sprinkled pleasure and happiest in mirth.

She had always known him, the king, in her lifetime
in him existed a happiness everlasting some might say
A feeling swept over her, at nights
A tender caress across her body as she lay.

He became an elegant gliding lotus bird, that grasped her
They flew the universe for hours at a time.
His gentle wings entwined themselves into hers
And whispered softly "I am yours, and you are mine"

His familiar music was now sown into the stars
And became anthem to their mystical path;
They danced in perfect togetherness,
Journeyed by their eternal threaded grasp.

Should it have been she tripped, or lost her stepping
Should she lose balance and begin to fall,
He would glide down and embrace her body with his
Carrying her close to him, so her descent was small

He would fly enough for two it seemed
his handsome nature and fine span of wings
Until finally she would regain her breath and compose herself
To continue alongside him, outstretching her wings.

Seahorses galloping at speed at their pleasure
from one shore to another in tireless abandon,
Messengers of faith to the love borne of the impossible
Uncurling promises of vows to be sung.

You are the sunshine upon my back,
And the strength of soft breezes offered for me to feel.
I have always loved you, forever and past eternity
I always have, my sweet love, and I always will.

FOLLOW ME INTO THE MYSTIC

This land where the venomous hounds unleashed
spit vitriol
and curve in audacious scorn.

But here is the world where dwells my buddha land
and there is freedom somewhere....

The land where I dwell is my Buddha land, my feet touch softly soil rich in lifetimes lived.
Now is my turn to change fortunes into gold,
Now is the time to unlock true fortunes of the world.

In timeless, ageless, countless fashion
without beginning and since kuon ganjo
Let go of layers dead, crisped with angst.....
Unfold the beauty that becomes apparent

Into my dreams and much further into reality, he stays constant in my heart, fills my day with
every fortune

.... Moving forward and further, towards the sun, because it always shines.....

She holds the tiger inside her
She is aflame with unbearable desire
She turns to face the arbitrary tongue....
and from deep inside she summons a passion so full,
so powerful, frighteningly loud it deafens the skies..........
and she roars.

TO LOVE HIM

I love him into the oldest
I love him into the wisest
Along the untamed
and through adventures yet to be explored.
"From starlight wonder along the mystical thread appears a love woven across oceans of
universe, of kuon ganjo

In him there is a radiance that shimmers across all the oceans and paints lustre into the sky
And I am evermore in love
I feel this beautiful man at every level.
Through every sound,
from every corner of the universe......
He emenates true magic, a mystical serum of honest affections I have always known.
He touches me when he smiles. His thoughts mingle into my own
He is the wonder I have never ceased to allow into my life.
He is the reason my heart grows in volumes and increases in the nectars that flows across the
invisible thread I have travelled along to find him....to get to him....day after day dream after
dream....life after new life....hour inside minutes singing to the seconds that linger in turn as I
wait for him, have waited for him, and,

Soft taunting voices cry out" was it worth it ", The Winds of Dubiety question :
"If it means my life has become enriched
If it signifies that the world
Has reason to rotate
If you want to know why my heart misses beats then patters away as if drummed by some
mystical palm
If it is that colours have created pastels of offspring never before existed
That by looking upon this man I visualize a loving masterpiece
I cannot keep from gazing
If I found true beauty that forms as this nectar pure and unadulterated, drunk heartily by us both
inked in such sweetness I discover from his pen to my own heart,
oh if it is to be loved unconditionally and exist in this moment to be free and glide alongside him

To hold on tight as the world turns

and dance the eternal of a song only lovers know, sung at the beginning before any beginnings existed,

If it means the stars form each night and the planets align in the harmony of his name....yes yes YES

It was worth it.

Yes! It still is worth it.

He is the breath I breathe

He is the kisses I feel on my skin, across my face, upon my lips....

He provides the comfort at such long distance he is closer now than I have ever known

Yes he is my love.

He is my truelove along the mystic

Yes it is worth it and it is always worth it.

Please go now winds of dubiety, I know my heart and its place is home, firmly inside the magnificence that keeps my truelove alive

You may blow strong, and continue across our horizons

but his heart is bigger

It cannot be compared.

I am a fortunate woman to be his muse, there is worthiness here, yes it is worth it

Yes it is!!!

Yes!"

Nothing can deter me,

no one person, not a soul or thing,

I am yours on this, our everlasting promise.

No matter what keeps us from gazing into each others eyes nothing can falter our love as it deepens and grows,

It matters little because

If my heart beats inside yours and I feel you.

I have your arms all around me, I further my desires and this cause so great, and chant with my heart whole and fervent, we are together and meet, physically skin to skin, lips touching, smelling each other an fragrance to be admired that cannot be equalled of a love born of kuon ganjo.

I followed the hum of the universe, I always turned and trod,

skipping and moving to your works of art into the sensual atmosphere.

Your music swirls as a sensuous smoke all around me and will not leave because I will not let it.

It is the scent of the lovers.

When the sun passes the edge of the earth and sets fire to the horizon once more leaving hues of golden red and orange smoking into the secret ambience of twilight evening, twirling clouds of sweet lilac desires....I wait for you by the cradle of dawn.

Of sugar trees and the sun that rises behind their sweetness,
for all things of health and good fortune
as ripened by our faith in the mystic law.

He is where my sun sets......
as rare, as precious, as unique.....
againsty each sunrise,
alongside every sunset.....

10,000 seahorses have carried upon their manes my messages to his shores across the limitless
plains of kuon ganjo.

I pick up the threads of hope, golden braided silver that glisten into the sun, and clasp them
into unbreakable loops around my fingers......
These I hold onto, a determined song of eternal gratitude and splendour
With a heart as full as an ocean unable to break

Golden fortune rises from the east, each morning, to match the sun and it becomes apparent
that winter does turn into spring. I travelled a million lifetimes along this mystical thread to
be at your side.
You do not know me,
But I will not be gone.

Wonder true that as we are fervent in our prayers and with a passion so strong in my heart for all things good that it is indeed a quest of the universe...... to endure the many occasions where connection has been blighted, many silences as all manner of power and correpondence played havoc incompleting our conversations, unable to connect, yet through unwavering strength and belief in one another we strive forward and move through, seeing each other at the end of each prolonged journey. A great light, a majestic, bright, beautiful light. That in itself is worth it.

It may try, and vy with sly brothers,
To taunt and hurt me, push me and poke at me,
but nothing can stop me...

"Loki leave me now, I am too tired and not interested anymore
10 daughters cannot tempt him further
They do not hurt me either
Let them know".

"because in the legend of gypsy wild roams a fortune dancer,
her hair aflow with the mystical breezes and her body bathed in gold.
There is a king upon his jewel encrusted mountain......
…..... he taps a drum that resounds in song about the universe
heard in every corner, he is where the sun sets west...."

Of heart connection and such mystical wonder throughout the hum of the universe, she had always danced to the unique sound of his drum...
He felt her move,
or so they say, because of course,
She had loved him into the wisest,
the oldest,
the untamed
and everything she never knew
and further more, she was in him,
everything he had ever known.

The land where I dwell is my Buddha land
My feet touch softly, soil rich in lifetimes lived,
Now my turn accentuates time to change fortunes into gold.

Of arbitrary tongue and pained wall
Stand yourself between us

The devils lurk in dirty shadows
Slinking softly
sidling quietly
But I will not entertain them
In myself I shower clean incessant whims

And return from the winds that blow with burdensome force

I promised to love you into the wild
and the untamed
And into the magnificent

There are those winds that blow the coldest
And from when it had rained upon the gates of dubiety
Fierce winds blowing against rages of defiance
forming a smoke of unchanged beauty
Only ever deepening
unchained and open passions.

And I sense you all around me into the furthest insecurities
far out reaching the places I cannot bear to be.

You are in everything
I am so grateful that you smile
because it shines.

There is much to do
And I am happy we marry our hearts to be together

Finding the mystical connection across the universe is to discover even buddhas fall in love.

A LIGHT OF SHEER GOLDEN HONEY

Within him there shines a light of golden honey
He holds the lantern high

I found my way
One morning before sunrise

And I sensed he was all around me into the furthest insecurities
far out reaching the places I could not bear to be.

By ten stretches of the mind and something more
I had no idea of how much magic
Could spill from an overfilled heart
the day the sun eclipsed
...... and I am stolen inside me
A feeling that will not leave
Could I shake him free against idle winds
carrying affections....
Would I wish to.....

In him there is enough light he holds the lantern high, I find my way....
In him the lantern burns fervently,
In him chants the universe,
the song of the sky in magnificence
In him is found the dance
I have felt within me always.
He speaks words that sparkle gold
Guiding me, holding his torch so bright
I find my way.

THE KUON GANJO PRINCE and THE LOTUS PRINCESS
(UPON THE CRYSTAL MOON)

A journey that has begun across the horizon
Adventures upon golden paved pathways appear
Threads of somewhere
Happening in timeless union
Along the mystic …..

The crystal moon gazed upon nocturnal oceans
Rippling against midnight
Bathed in quiet starlight

1000 questions posed as she leant against the sails…

"In the stillness and quiet of your mind
The wisest words are often heard"
She had heard him sing

The sky turned a flowing indigo
Streamed with pastels of green, silver
When he mysteriously wove him self into her dreams
Imperceptible by day
And the sonnet of their pledge was relived,
Re dreamed….

He softly spoke;
"I know the universe has everything we need
Await me therefore upon tomorrow innocent and golden
I will appear.....

I will forever be part of your dreams"

And so she asked,
" from the sweetness of angels
You have brought me to my knees

With you such beauty I have not known"

At this moment
The skies unfolded in lilac and soft ocre
As she continued,

"And I dare to seek your presence

You are a prince to the eternal sunrise
And I love you evermore

And we knew this journey would be trepid
Yet never feared the unknown
evenso
How do we leave what we know behind"

He smiled,
" follow me into the heart of the impossible"

As he leaned forward he whispered,

….it exists……"

And when he clapped his hands and the entire universe lit up.

It is into the eyes of the beloved the true buddha then appears.
To look into the eyes of the lover is to see the heart of the mystic unfold....

"He is of guidance and brilliance
In flight, magnificent charge he grasps of the skies
And leaves perfumed smoke
In colours no more visible unless to those lovers

Who have travelled since kuon ganjo

In union born again and again I pledge to be.....
Always his, my heart as full as the sea
I am touched by his very presence
inside, to be engaged by the everlasting honey of my soul.
Offer my love in abundance therefore sweet sister moon this evening
upon your silver sky,
and seek him to know my songs.......

Without doubt none there are, to compare to my love.

It is into the eyes of the beloved the true buddha then appears.
To look into the eyes of the lover is to see the heart of the mystic unfold

WHEN THE TIGER JOINS THE HEART OF THE HUNTED GYPSY.....
I MAKE MY DANCE FOR YOU

Can he know of my love truly, does he recognize my feelings and feel his own in connection with these,
I love you into the oldest,
the wisest,
the most untamed,
and if I have hurt a million times,
my darling it was a worthy cause to get to this point with you.

...... you rise within me, in subtle gentle warmth, a flourish of nerves and excitement, that burns
inside me yet leaves no trace of pain, my skin unhindered and my inner body without marks.....
these are not the feelings of anxious mind, uneasy, unrested......they belong to the world of
rapturous joy, sensuous wonder to be explored and believed, licked and nibbled and teased......
Your lips against my skin. Upon my lips, I need you, I yearn for you.... the world can stop a
while, and I breathe.......with you it makes sense, it happens, its there.

On finding myself alone, waking without you,
you are not there no matter how much I look,
my arms reach out....

On closing my eyes the fairies of ForeverWorld visit me again
I had often lived there when time mattered nothing,
Riding high, 3 abreast on the backs of lilac gold scaled dragons
of fireless breath,
Dancing to magic played upon the natural vibrations of the forests.....
they sing of love released......
of whispers in the Mystic when our music began,
where I vowed to never leave you
to always listen for the beat of your drums
where you clapped your hands, and before me the entire universe was alight
As if the sun had woven flames and connected with each adjacent sun
And created a world alight in flames of magnificent colours that have not yet reached
us, but I dream in them, when I dream of you.

I hear the song of the Beloved
Crystal countenance of beautiful sister moon emenates,
thousands of kisses raining sweetly upon us both....

I catch each of them with hands clasping each magical embrace
licking my lips to taste your beauty
To be without is to live where the rains pours constantly.....

My love my love. .. Once more he returns my beautiful man.
Inhabits my dreams sings songs lyrically penned from his heart
in inked perfection to mine own.....
He lights the world and does he know how my body pulses in inflamed passions.

I will shoulder the storm with you,
In you my heart belongs,
And it soars to the resonance of your love that surges through me
Although much turbulence persists now
and I am vulnerable
and I so very much wish to make peace
and search the places that allow us comfort
In forest enchantment and oceans of unknown discovery
From the storms of tumultuous rage and disruption,
until the moon's calming grace in white and silver,
when the sky turns to gold and burns brightly at sunset
and what had been confused reveals clearer, softer breezes of understanding.....

A whisper from the mystic
a crescendo from my wiser friends
whose tiny bodies dance in unity with heavens open embracing rains as amrita

Our prayers are theirs
they dance on into nightimes endless, of an age where they were born, timeless
Each with arrow poised and target enhanced
they cannot miss,
and disappear as fast as they arrive at the possibility of disbelief.....
because if not for you, my loving man then tell me who, if not you.....
then who......

that our connection may shine in brilliance ….
secrets between each betrothed since kuon ganjo,
A gentle murmur, from your lips across how many miles and years of mystical thread
"I love you"
Sweet promise of a thousand lifetimes, if not in this one, then the next......
"I love you still, because I always have"….

And we will never be tamed as we had always vowed, promises of togetherness and with
all that may stand between us, only you could offer me solace as the fire surfaces within,
encapsulates my body, pushes me to clifftop edges and urges me
places I do not want to be.......
Playing with my fears, teasing me relentlessly.......

I do not know these feelings so well but bow in reverence to every boulder that has appeared
unmovable, because to stand alone is a victory unsurpassed, and my faith is unwavering....
and to know you my beautiful man, to live with you in my heart, to have faith enough to
know you allow my heart to rest within the endless chambers of your own, m that beats with
powerful echo throughout the universe..... a pulse I had heard so often and drew such comfort
from …..

I am yours upon an everlasting promise
I am the soft breezes I wish to allay your worries
Until my fingers can run through your hair...tenderly touch your face..
.ripple across your skin, until such time as my body honours yours
with such humble ecstasies found amongst the undefeated lotus birds
bejewelled in colours unseen beyond dreams, highest of flight unwavering in their
conviction......I am the cool night time fresh breeze that refreshes the residue of dry dusty heat.
I allow my heart to be contained safely within yours my king of lifetimes passed.....
I feel the contents of your own beautiful heart spill into mine,
sweet intimate nectar of vows pledged from one love to another.
As I offered as the beginnings dawned on the birth of the first horizon. .....
I was yours betrothed and waiting.
If we could not be...
then as we promised against backdrops bloodied and crazed, threatened, harnessed by
contemptuous limitations of societies, pious and cruel.....

If not in this one, my love, then I will find you on the next......
because as promised, if not for you, then who......
who......

I will find you upon the next sunrise.....

OF PASSIONS AND HEARTS RENDERED IN LOVE

One man of passion and romance, of reality and deeper understanding,
my friend and husband,
my betrothed since before beginnings evolved into sunrise...
bringing truth and goodness to a world incomprehensible,
brushing away tears kissing my face dry....
sense finally arrived on the day true magic manifested where I lay eyes upon you.

Up into the silver moon countenance,
from the mystical scent of lovers,
Everything I ever searched for became the Known
In flight for the fearless,
To speak for the Unspoken
In him to see into the eyes of the beloved,
Was to reveal the Passion of the Mystic.

Wrap me up into your arms of velvet lilac surprise,
Allow me to fall into you, your body,
That knows me...........

ON GOLDEN MOON RISING

Bring me my love across the horizons of everlasting dreams..
.radiant in your cool white wonder shine on sister moon,
over my prince of a thousand lifetimes,
and golden moon rising I promise my honest affections
against all pain and agony..
.allow my sweet prince to know my heart to know of my love....
until the next blue moon when we renew vows a thousands years old......

ALLOW THE TIGER TO JUMP INTO MY HEART

Upon the back of a tiger fierce,
Haunted by the too close eagerness of a solo wolf, soft, hollow cry

He fills my head,
Swims in my mind,
Floods my heart
And appears as liquid around my eyes.

He is a thousand dreams,
He is a thousand heartbeats
Manifesting as promises held by the Mystic, in lilac gold.
Surrounded by a million lifetimes

I stand before him,
And he covers me in gold.
Speak the unspoken
Free deeply the scent of the beloved.
Know that I feel him,

Falling into the arms of the lover,
The heart of the mystic reveals
Treasures of untold fortunes........

It has been sung, in legends of gypsy wild
roams a fortune dancer
Her body bathed in his gold
moving in rhythm to the dance of the Untamed gypsy king
Some say it is possible to see
His heart beating closely into hers.......

There are those who say he knows her darkest secrets
And the reason she is terrified to tell,

That from years adrift
He can offer comfort to the cold and unease
And in these she will wait an eternity and forever
"Because in you my King "she sang
"I understood what I could not find,
And where love dwelled inside my heart
Was awakened
the moment your face shone into mine."

FOR LOVE PROMISED TO MY BETROTHED

Where love lies asleep in a body alive with dreams,
only to be awakened on first sight of your face
from the untamed dreams of the hunted gypsy
Reveal the courageous hearts believed by many
To contain the secrets of fortune endless.....

FOR MY ETERNAL GROOM

To my groom
And for my groom
my soul honours his
my world began to turn on sighting of him
To my groom
My beloved groom
I am promised to none other more
My heart embeds within his......

In union across everlasting oceans of serenity
And for my groom
to my groom
Who has awakened deep love inside
Now resonant throughout the universe

My heart joins yours
On an eternal journey
For my love whom offers himself
In comfort of my own life

Whisper the magic of fortunes revealed
"I am yours,
On an everlasting promise"
A determined song of eternal gratitude and splendour
With a heart as full as an ocean unable to break

Golden fortune rises from the east, each morning, to match the sun and it becomes apparent that winter does turn into spring.

Upon the back of a black lined silver tiger
Haunted by the eagerness of a wolf's cry
Along the river's the mystical winding......

He fills my head
Swims in my mind,
Floods through my heart,
And appears before my eyes

He is a thousand dreams
He is a thousand heartbeats
Surrounded by a million lifetimes
I stand beside him
He covers me in gold.

Warrior, partner me, I ask in simple whispers
Speak the unspoken
Free deeply the scent of the beloved.

He is countless in millions of heartbeats
Set free into each magnificent sunrise

In legends of gypsy wild
Where the untamed dance
And the hunted find solace against the universal hum

They bathe their limbs
from pools filled with lotus fusion.....

When he told me he loved me, the stars rang out the sweetest music I recognised since Kuon Ganjo
Their hearts beat in rhythm to the tunes of the mystic
Each perfect twinkle a heartbeat from the beloved.
Beyond the honey trees, hues in lilac, there is a river that flows with the sweetest nectar,
straight alongside the mystic......
In him there is everything to be certain of, and nothing to fear, he is my comfort, his love
embraces me like a million seas.

Of sugared fauna and the sun that rises behind their sweetness,
for all things of health and good fortune
as ripened by our faith in the mystic law.

He is where my sun sets......

..... a mystical thread fastened from her heart to his
on finding her truelove, the myoho princess assures herself,
within herself, that his footsteps are deeply engraved in the soil,
his knowledge fills the world,
the earth breathes and the breezes carry her love bounded westward to his side,
his music accompanies endless nightskies.....
the constellations bow in unison to the compositions moved alongside the turning wheels of life......
songs of the mystic so much greatly admired by the golden princess
this is undoubtedly a sure and profoundly desired, true and honest perception.
She has always heard him, always and always and evermore .....

OF MORE AND DISCOVERY

There is more to learn and to absorb and to discover....
Exciting and dangerous, unnerving, and the intrepid becomes known.
To venture onward is unavoidable but with cheered heart
and unshakable optimism it becomes an adventure into the unveiled mysteries,
waiting for discovery.......
and we observe change,
along the mystic where everything unfolds gradually according to our lifestates,
where we are, how we perceive.....

Where causes are planted watch as they grow,
possibilities unfold, opportunities flourish.....

OF MAGIC AND EMPATHS

In the world of the empath, newly founded,
it appears that brand new sensations arrive and spill over her body
embedding themselves into her bones,
flooding through her veins spreading colour s of indescribable beauty......
.ebbing and flowing as the tide might.....
sometimes with turblent spontaneity.......
sometimes quietly ascending, rippling into the skin,
as if fever has broken out, perspiring,
with a heart pounding as if wishing to burst from its cavity......
always inexplicable, often accompanied by panic.....
appearance is all brand new.....
there is something different to learn..

AS RARE, AS PRECIOUS, AS UNIQUE …..

Although your path forward suddenly became so dark
if you keep walking you will find a breaking in the sky
where the sunlight will relentlessly shine through.

For the sole purpose of loving you........
revealed is the heart of a loving mystical sage

Along the flow of the mystic
through the expanse of the unknown
appears a pathway to a journey
so unique,
it glitters as fortune might
when arriving unexpectedly......

You are a rare jewel that has been found in me finally,
a precious stone of priceless, ageless love
I am no longer adrift
and gift you my heart
place my hand in yours
and face forward.......

"How could I ever tame you
when all I want to do is ride aongside with you"
the gentle call of the king upon his mountain

He shows that even Buddhas fall in love,
and of this, I am certain.
Unfolding before me
fresh love born of the mystic
dreams lifted sweeter
from darkness that had filled themselves

Of her madness
who might know the magic
that turned around inside her mind.....
Revealing a glittering awkening
like a diamond
turning to gold

manifesting fortune jewels

opening upon his forehead
a most wonderful sight

Eyes that shone so brightly
Love is ever a universe unfolding,
And of faith and water
Flowing eternally
As rare as a turtle, adrift, one eyed,
You are as rare as a sought after gem.

Discovered by hands of the unique and beautiful.
Untold mysteries
Finally have sense, this is rare,
This is new...

As turbulence can discriminate
It cannot defeat me,
Let storms ride, and thunder climb the skies,
Lightening electrifies Earth's ceiling
but I cannot be shaken

Mountains are immovable
if they are rooted in strength
Unwavering against any weathers.

As rare as those who dance to a strange song
As rare, as the roar of the mystical Dragon
Firesong in full voice fulfilling me....

Whose fireless breath winds itself swirling across the lilac skies
In flight through the way of the vast skies around
All events unfold
Unveiled makes sense.
He is as precious as the ocean
As beauty is from the sun.

As my connected heart
Unlimited allows

It is warm upon the day,
and the sun is profoundest
No match for passions
Aflame.

If love is true
If it is but true

Then there is no suffer
To know
In the birth of love's first light

Felt first at heart
And once more
Throughout as rare, as precious.....

YOU ARE A THOUSAND DREAMS

You are a thousand names
You are a thousand men
You are a thousand dreams
You are a million heart beats
You make sense to the unbelievable
And I am the beauty seemingly beholden in you.
You are my friend
And finally I found you.
You are unlimited in your reason
You are imaginable to the bewildering
You are true magic in universal harmony
You are a masterpiece and I cannot keep from gazing
You are somewhere within me.

SENSE FINALLY ARRIVED ON THE DAY TRUE MAGIC MANIFESTED, WHERE I LAY EYES UPON YOU

Take me into the brighter side
Where he lives
At reflection at morning and evening
I sing in tune with him

And the world harmonizes

I hear him in everything
I see him everywhere

As rare as a love borne of Kuon Ganjo
Know me again
A call echoed against nightimes upon nightimes

I am yours upon an everlasting promise
I have sung again and again endlessly

I am the soft breezes I wish to allay your heated worry
Until my fingers can run through your hair
Tenderly touch your face

ripple across your skin,
until such time as my body honours yours
with such humble ecstasies found amongst the undefeated lotus birds
now restored and ready for flight
bejewelled in colours un seen beyond dreams,
highest of flight unwavering in their conviction....

I am the cool night fresh breeze that refreshes the residue of dry dusty heat
I allow my heart, within my own self, to be contained safely inside yours
because you are my king of lifetimes passed

I feel the contents of your own beautiful heart to spill into mine,
sweet intimate nectar of vows echoed throughout kuon ganjo

You who manifest the entirity of the universe into his being
You flood through me

Vows pledged to one another
as I offered as the beginnings dawned on the birth of the first horizon

I was yours and betrothed, I waited......and promisedI always would

you are as treasured as the jmystical texts that cool my fevered questions
you as precious as a piece come adrift in an ocean with no limits
with a horizon golden and in view
you are the way home.
You reached for me......
And through roiling waters, I recognised your hand.....

Against backdrops bloodied crazed, drowning, threatened, harnessed by contemptuous
limitations of the pious and cruel.......
You are as precious and as rare

You exist in the very meaning of love
And they may have prised us apart
pulled you from my arms

but my eyes spoke my heart across a connection they could not break
and to you I cried
"if not in this one, my love,
then I will find you on the next".....

Sense finally arrived on the day true magic manifested where I lay eyes upon you
Best friend and truelove.
Of passion and truer romance,
from dreams into reality
Stands before me my friend and confidante,
husband, bringing truth and goodness into a world, incomprehensible....

brushing tears from my face,
Smiling into me when I thought I might fall into the colder madness
Sense most certainly arrived on that beautiful day.

IN HONOUR OF A HUSBAND FOUND ACROSS THE GOLDEN HORIZON

*If it were possible to travel the jewelled dragon back to follow the chimes
and be near you,
I would gladly respond.*

*His Eagle tongue cries from the wild,
The song of the untamed,
A call along the mystic
It is the most beautiful sound in the whole world.*

*Your voice upon mine
A silver river into the universe.*

*From the heart of the pure
We have touched this place before
In you, I know.*

*To swim alongside your voice
Is the most enchanting journey I could know
Sense arrived the day we met,
The universe came alive
and my heart lit up.....*

*Of wonder and gracious offerings
I knew your song
I followed your voice.......I heard you play.....*

*To swim alongside your voice
Is to know magnificence
Is to honour the man of a thousand dreams
Of a thousand lifetimes
A million heartbeats*

you are a masterpiece and I cannot keep from gazing,
I can nothing more but renew my daily vows
In love and everlasting devotion
Of honour and gracious wonder

I bathe in your gold
You paint me eternal
And ride the jewelled tapestry backed Eagle dragon
From my world to yours

Your voice upon mine
A silver river into the universe.
Watch us spread our wings
Take flight, again and always, in eternal migration across the universe
Into anywhere
Your arms firmly around me
I can go everywhere, I have no more fear,
My eyes do not feel the salt,
My heart is once more complete.

Let them hunt and plunder, they might trip us, and we may fall,
but know your hearts, remain forever untamed.......
Along the night of the unknown
Fear may seek but receive no company.

Rise up in a thousand different colours, unfold your wealth.

✰✰

THE END